THE RAT
WORSHIPPER

T0158746

THE RAT WORSHIPPER

in the nick of time

Based on a True Story

G.W. Rennie

iUniverse, Inc.
Bloomington

The Rat Worshipper
in the nick of time

iUniverse books may be ordered through booksellers or by contacting:

iUniverse
1663 Liberty Drive
Bloomington, IN 47403
www.iuniverse.com
1-800-Authors (1-800-288-4677)

ISBN: 978-1-4620-4493-1 (sc)
ISBN: 978-1-4620-4494-8 (ebk)

Printed in the United States of America

iUniverse rev. date: 09/20/2011

Epiphany **def:**
(feeling) a sudden realization of great truth

To my dear niece, Jessica

CONTENTS

Preface

The Rat Worshipper is about the earlier years of my life—it is based on true events around the rat. Some of these events that I get into are quite unusual and controversial. You may judge some of these events as being somewhat questionable, but I do try to leave it open for contemplation and conjecture based upon my own personal experiences.

Imagine dimensions that go beyond the outer limits of the senses that we possess—sight, sound, touch, smell, and taste. These limited senses are what make up the world we know and give us the ability to interact with the world around us. What if there is something more? What if there is something our five senses cannot perceive?

I have often wondered about the subject of divine intervention. I am talking about certain events that unfold that, if followed, could lead to your very salvation. We have all heard of other stories around these unusual happenings, be they fiction or truth. I do not know too much about the latter.

My own experiences with the unexplainable ultimately led me to writing *The Rat Worshipper*. These events are what made me the way I am today. I have often wondered why my life turned out the way it did. I did not ask for the rat to be a part of my life, but it appeared to me that this was inevitable. I did not make this choice—it was made for me by something that seems beyond belief.

When I found out about other groups of people from all over the world who share the same kinds of interests as I do, I was inspired to write about my adventures with the rat. Others held conflicting opinions about my particular views and interests around the rat. I am not trying to make any claims here. It is up to you to decide. However, this may really make you think of something that is far greater than us.

Everyone has a story that deserves to be told—here is mine.

Chapter 1

The Encounter

My first childhood memory takes place when I was around three years old. My immediate family and I lived in an apartment building in Halifax, Nova Scotia, in what were called PMQs. These were permanent married quarters for military families that served in the Canadian armed forces.

In those days, the Canadian Navy was known as the Royal Canadian Navy. In his younger days, my father served for many years. The quarters we lived in were for families that needed to be accommodated when traveling to certain bases to continue training; my father was training in both combat and peaceful exercises that are important to the country's defense and security.

Since we primarily lived on Canada's west coast, we traveled east to Halifax, Nova Scotia, from Victoria, British Columbia, and back. When my father would take holidays, our usual method of travel was by car and camper. We would all trek across Canada and visit different campsites and parks. We enjoyed everything we did as a family, and

I developed a love for the outdoors. Camping, fishing, and hiking were some of these activities that we enjoyed.

I was too young the first time we traveled across to remember too much. My father drove us across Canada four times! That is a lot of driving—crossing Canada and back from coast to coast. We did this because it was so much fun. We did have our difficulties, however. When we were tenting at a campground, we were caught in a deluge and everything got soaking wet. This was before we got the camper.

When we were driving around one of the great lakes in Ontario, my brother Warren needed to relieve himself on the side of the road one hot, muggy summer's evening. He was instantly covered with large black mosquitoes as soon as he stepped out of the car door. There were five of us, including my dad, my mom, and my two older brothers. This first crossing led us all into the PMQ apartments for the first time.

This is where my story gets a little unusual. On this first trip to Halifax, my life went down a different road, as a result of the following events. We took up residence at the permanent married housing complex in Halifax, Nova Scotia.

The building complex was suffering from a rather large rat problem. It was a species of Norway rat. The rats were so big that conventional traps did not work on these beasts. They were as big as cats, and special box traps were needed to catch them.

My brother Scott was with a group of friends when they came across a large black rat that seemed to be really agitated about something. When they saw what it was, they were aghast. A cat quivered in the corner of the building while the rat paced back and forth. Its tail was twitching wildly, and it was hissing and growling. It was growling at the poor cat that obviously did not want anything to do with the rat.

Scott does not remember what happened next. Maybe the cat finally took off while the rat gave chase. Perhaps something more graphic occurred that caused him to forget. My brother was only four or five at the time, but he was old enough to remember that part. I can remember everything in perfect detail with these rats from beginning to end—even though I was no more than two or three. The memory of these animals was etched into my brain forever.

I wandered down to the basement via the stairwell that led to the laundry room. I had a plastic water toy that resembled a water wheel—its red water basin was perched atop a yellow wheel with tiny buckets on the end. When you put water in the basin, it drained through a hole in the bottom to the little yellow buckets that made the wheel spin around. I do not remember why I went to the laundry room. Perhaps I needed a chair to stand on, but I was too small to drag a chair to the washroom in our apartment from the kitchen.

When I went into the basement, I was aware of a large cement sink and a chair that I could stand on to reach the faucet. My mother would take me down there to keep an eye on me when she did laundry. I knew that I could play with my water wheel toy without getting too wet.

The basement was completely empty, and I was too small to reach the narrow rectangular windows. The laundry room entrance was just an opening in the cement wall in the corner, kitty-corner to the dark-green stairwell door that entered the basement. A single clear bulb hung from a white cord about a foot from the middle of the untiled basement ceiling. It was overcast outside, but it was not raining.

I am guessing it was late morning or early afternoon, because it was daylight. I was too young to tell time, but this is the time of the day I seem to remember. I proceeded to play with my toy while standing on the chair in front of the sink so I could reach the taps. The water made a trickling noise while I was playing, which no doubt triggered the following event. I was too young to understand or comprehend it, but I will never forget what happened.

When I was finished playing, I went into the basement and I was greeted by the sight of a large black rat in the middle of the basement floor! It was staring right at me. Those black piercing eyes are what I remember the most. It was perfectly motionless, perfectly still. An overpowering, primordial fear swept through me. I was sure that I was going to die.

I threw my back up against the wall and froze for a moment, wondering what the rat was going to do next. Thoughts were flying through my mind. *Where did it come from? What is it doing here? Was it here when I came in? Are there any more of them? Why isn't it doing anything? Is it going to kill me? Is it going to eat me?*

All I wanted to do was play with my toy—I had never asked to be confronted and terrorized by a big black rat! After a moment or two, I found the courage to slowly creep along the wall toward one corner of the basement to the door and freedom. The rat was directly between me and the stairwell door.

When I got to the next wall, where the door was, I noticed that the rat did not move. It didn't twitch a muscle. I couldn't even see it breathe. When I got within arm's reach of the door, I could feel the rising anticipation of my escape—and then I ran upstairs as quickly as I could!

I developed a fear of rats after this took place because I did not have the cognitive reasoning at the time to comprehend the events around this encounter. This fear eventually turned into fascination. When I was older, I reflected on this encounter from time to time.

I was wondering why the rat did not do anything to me other than make an appearance. It had me right where it wanted me. I was quite literally trapped like a rat. The rat had turned the tables on me and it looked even bigger than me! I realized later that the sound of the water might have attracted the rat.

It may have been thirsty and was waiting for me to leave so it could drink the water in the sink. There was no water in the sink before I turned on the taps—it was bone dry. It may have been a chance meeting—a coincidence of which many more would follow. I wondered why the rat walked out into the middle of the empty basement floor in broad daylight!

Since rats do not behave this way, this has always been a mystery to me. Why did it do that? Perhaps it just didn't see me as a threat. Maybe it happened for a reason in the grand scheme of things. Whatever the reason, this event led me down a different road. The road would eventually lead me into the Twilight Zone—and it would change my life forever.

During my childhood trips across Canada, we were always on the move. We ended up living in the PMQ housing in Colwood, British Columbia. On the other side of the Esquimalt Harbor, there was an area called Belmont Park. A green army bus would pick up my father in front of our house to transport him to the destroyer escort ship that he served on.

A blue boat ferry service was set up on the Colwood side of Esquimalt Harbor to take the men to the navy docks. It was a shorter, easier method of travel than the old army buses. I used the blue boat service when I was old enough to serve, but that's another chapter of my life.

We lived in a white and red house that looked like most of the other houses. When I started kindergarten at John Stubbs Elementary School, I got to know all the other base brats. The school was not too much different from the ones on the other side of the fence. The only differences were that you did not know as many people who were not part of a base community and you did not start the school day without saying the Lord's Prayer. I have always remembered it.

> *Our father, who art in heaven*
> *Hallowed be thy name*
> *Thy kingdom come, thy will be done*
> *on earth, as it is in heaven.*
> *Give us this day, our daily bread*
> *and forgive us our trespasses,*
> *as we forgive those who trespass against us.*
> *And Lead us not into temptation, but*
> *deliver us from evil,*
> *for thine is the kingdom,*
> *the power and the glory,*
> *forever and ever,*
> *Amen.*

Chapter 2

The Summer Cabin

When I turned six, my aunt and uncle on my mother's side acquired a summer cabin on the Sunshine Coast. You could only get there by boat because there were no roads. It was just the trees, the sky, the mountains, and the lake.

The boat trip took forty-five minutes in a fully loaded sixteen-foot aluminum boat with a nine-horse outboard and two families onboard! The cabin came to be one of my favorite places because it was far away from civilization.

On our first visit to the cabin, there was a big log on the shoreline next to a big rock bluff in a cove. We tied up to a steel ring that was bored into a log in front of the cabin. Everybody slept in the large, one-room cabin for the first summer.

It didn't seem very roomy with two big families in there. There were twelve of us with my new baby sister, Maggie; my aunt and uncle; and their four girls. My cousins all had long blonde hair that went down to their waistlines.

If my cousins weren't skiing in Whistler, British Columbia, when they lived in North Vancouver, they were traveling to destinations like Europe, Egypt, and Africa. They learned French and were quite affluent. They always had interesting stories from their adventures.

My uncle was an executive at IBM and earned a six-figure salary. He also had an interest in the native arts, which were everywhere in his home and workplace. At my oldest cousin's place in Richmond, two totem poles lead into their residence. My uncle gave them the totem poles as a housewarming gift and wedding present after she married a banker. My cousin is an elementary schoolteacher, but they don't have any children of their own.

The next year, there would be a bigger A-frame cabin built close to the original cabin—and closer to the bluff with the jetty that extended into the lake. The original cabin is still there as a guesthouse. My mother's younger sister and her family would often stay there until their marriage broke up a few years later.

In August 1970, when I was seven years old, I had another disturbing encounter on our second visit to the cabin.

A family with two sons—one about my age and an older brother—was building their own cabin just up the trail from ours. The Templetons had a sailboat anchored in the harbor; I assumed it was theirs because there were no other cabins in the immediate area.

After arriving at the cabin, my aunt and uncle checked on the neighbor's cabin because they were arriving within the next few days and it had not yet been completed. They were set to arrive within a few days to apply the finishing touches to the cabin. It was up on a smaller rock bluff that had a better view of the lake, but they had to go down a network of stairs to get to the dock and the boat.

I wondered why our cabin was completed first, because they had started before my grandfather. It probably took them longer because of the trip up and down those stairs. The cabin was basically built, but there were no window panes put in yet.

The openings were covered with thick plastic to keep out the weather. The interior still needed some walls to be closed up where the insulation was tacked in, but the roof had been completed. What my aunt and uncle discovered turned out to be quite shocking.

Apparently, over the winter, their cabin had been overtaken by what appeared to be hundreds—if not thousands—of rats! The floor was completely covered in rat feces and urine. In the corners of some of the walls, the insulation had been ripped out and was being used as nesting material. All the rats were gone by this time because of the warmer weather, but the scope of the situation was quite remarkable. I've never seen an infestation like this—even to this day.

My aunt and uncle's house faced directly out onto the lake. There was a loft upstairs that required an almost vertical wooden stepladder to get to. It was often too hot up there to sleep because of the indoor propane lamps that were always lit when the sun went down, or from the heat of the day. Mostly because of the lamps though.

In front of the A-frame was a covered patio, and a dining area was outside to the right. On the left was a set of stairs at the side of the cabin that went down to the jetty. In the middle of the patio, a tree was growing through the center of the floor and out through the roof. Next to the tree was an old green hand pump where we got our water from the lake. We often had to fill this bucket because there was no running water for the sink inside the kitchen.

We could hear activity on the roof when we slept in the loft until the screened-in enclosure underneath the cabin was put in with six bunks inside for us younger kids. We could sometimes hear rats running along the flat part of the roof. We ended up sleeping in the screened-in enclosure underneath the cabin after it was completed.

When it was time for bed, we did not have to worry about climbing the steep stairs in the loft or carrying a flashlight in the middle of the night. The rats on the roof wouldn't keep us awake at night, but they were scaring my cousins. We still had to watch out for rats, skunks, and raccoons because they sometimes inhabited the space underneath the floorboards.

My aunt, uncle, four cousins, and the rest of us went to work about cleaning up as much of the mess that we could. Of course, all of us younger kids were more interested in swimming, waterskiing, and hiking along the trails than days of cleaning up. Our visits were typically a couple of weeks, so a day or two to help out our neighbors wasn't too much of a burden, especially if everybody chipped in.

If the new A-frame had not been completed, we would have waited until the following year to visit because the close quarters were a little uncomfortable. Nobody had any privacy. I always wondered how much work it was for my grandfather ferrying all the tools and materials by boat to the cabin site. It must have been quite an undertaking.

Although my grandfather was a fisherman by trade, he was also an accomplished carpenter and builder. My mom recently took me to Steveston in Richmond, British Columbia, to show me one of the houses that he built that is still standing and in good repair. It was close to the Steveston docks where he once owned a boat-building business that was connected to the fishing industry. He acquired the business after the Japanese were interned during the Second World War.

There were plenty of activities for us at the cabin. My favorites were waterskiing, disc board tiding, windsurfing, and sailing. Sometimes we hiked from one end of the lake to the ocean to search for oysters that we would barbecue back at the cabin, but you had to take the boat from our cabin to the part of the lake that led there.

In the meantime, my aunt and uncle took the boat to the location on the lake where we parked our vehicles to go into town for supplies. I opened one box that contained the rat poison. I ended up getting some of the powder on my hands and was instructed by my father to thoroughly wash them under the hand pump.

Any night we got together with the Templetons at their cabin, we would take propane torches, kerosene wick lamps, or flashlights on the trails because it was always pitch black out and we could easily get lost.

Other cabins dotted the lake. On a calm night you could hear people talking across the lake. A lot of the cabins were connected by trails. We became good friends with the Templeton family over the years.

The morning after the cabin had been cleaned and baited with the poison and traps, my aunt came down the trail in a panic after checking on the cabin. A rat was caught in one of the traps. It wasn't dead yet, but it was causing a bit of a racket as it struggled with the trap. A number of us went to take a look. My aunt used a small stepladder to look on top of the cabinet inside. We were all curious to see what was up there.

When I climbed the ladder, I could see the rat breathing heavily. It was facing me with a small pool of blood by its head. Looking into its eyes brought back the memory of my first encounter with the rat. It was like looking at a reflection of my own primordial fear.

Seeing the rat was like looking at myself as a three-year-old kid. I could see the terror in its eyes. It was very disturbing. I couldn't stop thinking about it. For compassionate reasons, it was promptly put out of its misery. We were humane about it.

After that experience, I started to gain a sincere interest in rats. I began doing research on the animal after we got home to Vancouver Island. Movies, documentaries, and books about them became a major focus in my life that would eventually lead to me keeping them as pets.

I found out that some people actually kept them as pets. I often asked my parents if I could get one, but the response was always no—partly due to our own experiences with them.

One of the things I looked forward to when we went home after the holidays was visiting my grandparents on my father's side of the family. My grandfather was actually my step-grandfather because my dad's real father had passed away years earlier. I never did get to know him because I wasn't born yet, my grandfather passed when my father was only eleven years old. From what I heard from my father, he was quite the traditional individual in the Scottish ways.

He was very strict with my father. My father's interesting stories about my biological grandfather would make us laugh—like eating that traditional delicacy called haggis on the Scottish holiday he always celebrated. When my father told me about haggis, I was squeamish. I'm glad my father didn't make me eat it because he didn't like it either!

They lived in a small house in a rural part of the lower mainland, in Richmond. My grandmother always had a big bowl of ribbon candy for us when we visited. In later years, my grandmother got an infection in her leg because she was diabetic and ended up getting her leg amputated just below the left knee. It was kind of creepy for me to go see her after the loss of her leg, but it did not dampen her spirit. Since they were very friendly people and were always happy to see us, it didn't really bother me.

The visits were convenient for my dad since it was on the way home to Vancouver Island and it was an opportunity for him to keep in touch with his parents every year. It was also good for me and my siblings to know who they were. I was always grateful for this.

Chapter 3

The New House

We lived in the PMQ housing for the remainder of my father's stay in the military. Later in 1970, my father was watching an NHL hockey game with my oldest brother. It was the first game my brother Scott went to because he showed an interest in playing the game.

The first signs came about when my dad was bike riding with my brother a few days before the game. My brother Warren and I were still too young to ride the bigger bikes and couldn't keep up with my oldest brother's new ten-speed bike. My father became lightheaded and dizzy during the ride. He mentioned to my mother that he planned to see his doctor on the base the following week.

In the second period, my father suffered a heart attack. He had to be taken from the arena on a stretcher. He was only thirty-four years old, but he became medically unfit to serve in the military. The decision to have him honorably discharged due to medical reasons had to be made. Because he was an electronics technician, he was given the option of being hired as a civilian technician for the ships in the dockyard.

Every few years, the ships needed to come into huge docking bays that were closed off from the main body of water. The dry dock dam was put into place, and the large ships were supported by massive support blocks placed at the bottom of the dock bays. Work could be done on the hull, propeller, and other major parts of the ship, such as electronic overhauls and updates. Since my father was no longer a member of the armed forces, we could no longer stay in the PMQ.

We were given a grace period in which my father could find a new home while he worked as a civilian technician on the base. He spent some time in the hospital before he came home and a decision had to be made about open heart surgery. A triple bypass was quite new and the mortality rate was high until new procedures were introduced. Until surgery was scheduled, he was given heart medication and nitroglycerin tablets to control the angina attacks.

On New Year's Day 1971, we moved into a two-story house in Colwood. We would reside there for the next twenty-one years. It was a seven-year-old house with the upstairs part ready to occupy. The downstairs was still almost completely unfinished save for one bedroom on the northwest corner of the house. I would eventually occupy that room in the years that I lived there. My bedroom was the only one untouched by the renovation work downstairs.

Other than the laundry room, which was located at the bottom of the stairs and the downstairs bedroom, renovation work was planned for the rest of the house. A bedroom for my brother was added next to my future bedroom on the south side of the house. The basement would eventually be called the orange room due to the fact that the orange carpet we added. My father added a washroom next to the original bedroom and a music room for my mother with a stand up piano that she briefly used to teach piano lessons. His workshop led out to the carport on the east side of the house. My mother trained my sister Maggie once she showed an interest in playing the piano.

After we moved into the new house, I went to Colwood Elementary School. I had to make new friends and start a new life. The change was difficult for me. It was hard to say good-bye to my friends and neighbors, but it was an inevitable part of life. I did not like this kind of change; however, it opened up new doors that I had no choice but to accept.

The renovation took a few years because there were not many bedrooms to accommodate us. My two older brothers resided in the original downstairs bedroom during the renovation. There were three other bedrooms upstairs that my sister Maggie and I occupied.

Life on the outside was quite different from life at the PMQ housing because there was no longer a network of families. This was quite new to me, and I wondered why we never really got to know our new neighbors. We were there the whole time without really getting to know anybody. My father had an even tougher transition due to the change in his working environment and having to leave behind the life we all enjoyed. He still kept in touch with all of the people he came to know in the military.

When the renovation was complete, Scott moved into the new room while Warren stayed in the original room. It remained this way until Scott left for Alberta to look for summer work. Warren moved into Scott's old room because he liked more light on that side of the house, and I moved down to the original bedroom that had been occupied by Warren.

After Scott returned home due to a lack of work and experience, he moved into his old room where Warren used to stay before joining the Air Force. Maggie moved into my old room because it was bigger than hers—and her old room became a den for visitors. We did quite a bit of shuffling around in that house!

When I moved down to my new room, my parents got some new furnishings to go with it. I got a captain's bed with drawers and cabinets underneath to keep my clothes in. It was a tall bed that I practically had to jump into. My feet would not touch the floor if I was sitting on the mattress. I liked my room to be dark because it was on the north side.

The headboard was up against a ledge on the west side. I put an alarm clock and a radio on it. The ledge was about three or four feet off the bedroom floor and it ran along to the far corner of the bedroom. My bed was up along the south wall that was the back wall of Scott's closet in the added bedroom.

Like most youngsters, I liked to stay up late when I should be sleeping. My dad would often keep his bedroom door open and tell me to go back to bed when I tried to sneak out at night to watch TV when I slept upstairs. The move gave me a little more freedom—as long as I kept quiet downstairs.

When I turned twelve, I wanted to get a pet. My parents ended up getting me a black lab that I named Nippy. I named him Nippy because he kept biting me! I had to wear a thick jacket every time I went to spend time with him in the back yard. The yard was closed in by a high wooden fence that encompassed the whole property.

For two weeks, I spent every day with Nippy in the yard. I spent as much time as I could with him to bond, but no matter how hard I tried, he kept biting me. My parents were aware of my efforts to befriend my pet, but there seemed to be no progress. Two weeks later, Nippy was missing. I looked high and low, but I just couldn't find him. He just up and ran away.

I figured this was for the best because he didn't really get along with me despite how much I tried. I was upset about the loss, but the bond never came to be. On the bright side, I did not miss the biting. I guess he never really liked me.

Unlike rats, who bond very quickly to their new caretakers because they are much more social animals, they tend to bond to only one person. Nippy probably ran off to seek out the person he bonded with because he wanted nothing to do with me.

Shortly after he ran away, I was doing my paper route that I took over from Scott, when he went to Alberta to find summer employment. There was little work on the island, and the opportunities in Alberta were plentiful. I was riding my bike down the road on my route when I saw something in the middle of the road in the distance.

It looked like garbage strewn about in black plastic bags, but it turned out to be a black lab that had been hit by a vehicle. It resembled my lost pet Nippy, and it wasn't a pretty sight. When a car drove past as I rode by, the tires passing through the carcass made a sound I never want to hear again.

I had to pull my bike to the side of the road as the experience sickened me. That was the last time I got this kind of a pet—and it was not until this time that my parents allowed me to get my first rat!

Unlike Nippy, Camelot seemed to form an instant bond with me. He never did bite me, and he came to be a very attentive little guy. He was solid beige. In a short period of time, he came to be my best friend. I put his cage beside my bed and would leave his door open so he could get out and run around. I had to make sure that there were no electrical cords or clothes on the floor or he would chew through the cords or bite holes in my clothes. If anything, this gave me good cause to keep my bedroom neat and tidy!

I never realized just how social and friendly these animals were. If I'd known how social they were—particularly to their own kind—I would have gotten two. My parents would have allowed only one—no matter how much I begged. Since then, I have always kept at least two. If one was on the way to expiring, I would get another.

One benefit to having rats as pets is the notoriety you get from your classmates and friends. I would often invite my friends from Belmont Secondary School over to my house to show them my rat and the funny little tricks that I would teach him. Quite often while I was doing my homework, he would play with my hands, chew on my paper—I was constantly trying to make him stop—or sit on my shoulder.

I would ask him questions about my homework, and he always seemed to give me the right answer—or so it seemed. They were good little study buddies. I did get some strange looks from my teachers when I handed in my homework with the pages chewed. If I didn't complete my assignments, I could always say that my rat ate my homework! I always got a lot of laughs over that one—even from my teachers!

The only downside to rats is that they do not live that long. When Camelot passed away in 1977, he was just under three years old, which is about the average lifespan of a domestic rat. I was quite upset, but my parents found out what wonderful companions they make. They had no problem with me getting another one to replace Camelot.

Even though my new rat eased the loss somewhat, I realized that there could be no true replacement because of their personalities. I developed a new relationship with Whiskers; he was as entertaining as Camelot. He was even the same color.

When my father finished the renovation, there were different lengths of plywood strips that he placed in neat stacks against the carport wall.

Chapter 4

The Visions

In 1977, I received bad news about my dad's mother. The last remaining blood-related parent of my father had passed away. He had to make arrangements to go out to the mainland to make final arrangements and attend the funeral.

It was shortly after this that I started to have sleeping problems. The night terrors started after a bad concussion from ice skating—and they seemed to get worse. I was racing a kid down to the end of the rink after the Zamboni left the ice. Just before the end, the other kid pivoted around to skate backward to show off his skating skills.

I followed suit, but I tripped and smacked my head against the ice. I got up right away and continued to skate, but I felt really strange. Everyone on the ice seemed to keep blending into one another as they skated around. I knew there was something wrong inside my head so I went to the nurse's room. The nurse told me to follow her finger with my eyes, but I had trouble with it. My pupils were not responding properly to the flashlight.

My mother took me home to bed and was instructed to check on me every few hours. The next morning, I seemed to be fine, but I do not recall any of the conversations my mom had with me throughout the night. Everything was a total blank from the time I went to bed till I got up the next day. This was a problem for me because it was affecting my schoolwork, and my parents had to take me to a psychologist.

When they hit, I experienced paralysis and was not able to breathe or cry out. I was stuck between the world of consciousness and the dream world. I was totally conscious of what was happening around me, but was teetering on the edge of falling asleep, without completing the transition. In every episode, I thought I was going to die.

This must have had something to do with my head injury because of the frequent mild convulsions that accompanied these episodes. Suddenly, my hand or my foot would twitch violently and the spell would be broken. These episodes would often hit me in the morning after being woken up to go to school or as I would drift in and out of sleep.

One morning, when my mother woke me up to go to school, I slipped into an episode. I kept praying that my mom would come back to check on me. It felt like I was being squeezed to death by a large snake because I could not breathe. It seemed like a half hour of hell went by. I was wondering why it was taking so long for my mother to check on me. I would break out of the episode and discover that only two minutes had gone by! I guess when you are feeling like you are going to die, time slows down.

I learned to pay attention to one disturbing side effect. They were often accompanied by vivid nightmares or visions. There must have been some kind of psychic element to the episodes.

I had been suffering from these episodes for several years. When my mom woke me up for breakfast in 1980, I slipped into one of the episodes. It was accompanied by a deafening rumbling noise that went right through my bedroom. I thought we were having a major earthquake! I tried to shout, "What the hell is happening?" I was so startled that I couldn't even hear my own voice because of the noise.

I could see my window shattering, and the tiles in my ceiling were crumbling. Things were flying around my bedroom. This was really freaking me out, but as quickly as I slipped into the episode, I came out of it. All was well—just like that! The ceiling was fine, the window was intact, and nothing was amiss. I could not understand it.

I was convinced that we had had an earthquake. When I went up for breakfast, I asked my mom if we had just had one, but she said no. The following afternoon, I read in the newspaper of a powerful earthquake that had hit Naples, killing and injuring more than ten thousand people!

I knew my episode was related—and wasn't a coincidence. I was tuned-in to a disturbance on a psychic level from deep within the earth that prompted this vision. I had had a number of them in the past—and I just wanted them to go away.

I talked about some of the unusual visions with my psychologist. They were always accompanied by major disasters. A lot of them even came true as I was dying alongside other people.

I never talked about one particular episode because of its disturbing nature. I was drifting off to sleep shortly after my grandmother passed away.

Sometimes I could tell when I was about to slip into an episode. I always tried to avoid it by forcing myself awake, but sometimes it overcame me suddenly. I was drawn into the unbearable vortex of its relentless, terrifying effects. What accompanied this particular episode was the ghostly vision of my dead grandmother at the foot of my bed!

She was slowly rocking back and forth in her rocking chair, the stub below her knee was gently moving back and forth as she rocked. There seemed to be a vacuum in the room, and I couldn't breathe. There was a glow outside my window—an eerie flickering light like the Aurora Borealis that continued to grow brighter and brighter.

It was accompanied by the sound of this ominous, roaring noise like a fireball heading straight toward my window. It looked like my grandmother was trying to tell me something, but she was barely audible as a result of this increasing roar that was accompanied by the intensifying glow that was visible throughout the curtains.

At any moment, the fireball was going to burst through the window, instantly incinerating everything. However, as the curtains began to smolder from the intense heat, I suddenly broke out of the grip of the horrifying episode and bolted straight up in bed.

The room went dark, and my grandmother vanished. I was gasping for air, and the sheets were soaking wet from the sweat of fear that I had just experienced. This was the worst episode that I have ever encountered. I had an insufferable feeling that I was going to die. I anticipated this as a vision of my own fiery death!

I was grateful for the sessions with the psychologist over the next several months. I think I would have gone quite mad if it wasn't for them. I rarely suffer from these episodes anymore as I might get one a year. In the past, I was experiencing them at least once or twice a week. Better yet, I rarely get those terrifying visions anymore. They were slowly killing me.

The last significant episode I experienced that was accompanied by these visions was about my brother Warren. I was in Halifax for a radar operator's course in 1986.

Chapter 5

My Brother Warren

Warren didn't seem to have a care in the world, but he squinted with a nervous twitch. Warren was the strongest of the three of us when we were in our final years at Colwood Elementary.

He could lift the rear end of a car's tires off the ground when he was only twelve! I don't know how he did it. I never could, and nobody else could either. He had a set of weights that he got for Christmas that he was always working out on.

Warren had the temperament and strength of Superman. He was unbreakable, and everybody liked him. Warren played on the high school rugby team. He was a formidable force on the field and was one of the team's best players, but he quit shortly after chipping one of his teeth during a scrimmage.

Warren was outgoing and social. He volunteered as a counselor at a summer camp every year when we weren't at the cabin. He was a credit to the community. He owned a house in Winnipeg when he served in the Canadian Air Force.

He had everything going and was my role model. We always wore the same style of clothes when we were younger, and I always tried to be like him. Scott pushed me around a lot, but I know it was all in fun. I have always looked up to him too.

In May 1986, I visited Warren on my way to my course. The woman renting a suite told me he wasn't home and would not be back for a few days or so. Disappointed, I decided to proceed to Halifax.

Two and a half months later, I was seized by an episode as I was waking up that I had not experienced in a few years. What accompanied this one was a droning noise in the background, like a car motor idling. What I saw was a gradually increasing mist in the distance against a pitch black backdrop.

As the mist grew larger and brighter, I could begin to see a silhouette of a dark figure arising out of the middle of the mist, sitting in what looked like one of those bucket seats from a small car. I was drawn to the figure. As I drew closer, I sensed that the figure was somebody I knew—someone very close to me. What was particularly disturbing was that the individual in the chair was deceased.

I saw the image of my father looking down on the figure. He looked like he was experiencing great grief. It occurred to me that the individual in the chair had taken his own life from the expression I read on my father's face.

The drone of the motor in the background began to increase in volume as I drew closer. Just before I could see the face of the person in the chair, my head began to spin. The noise got louder and louder. My head felt like it was going to explode. I was enveloped by a very dark cloud and experienced the sensation of falling into a deep void. I broke out of the episode and sat up in bed. I said, "No! He wouldn't do that."

My two roommates had gone home when they finished their course on Friday, so I was alone. *Who is he? Is it one of my brothers? A close family friend?* I had not had a chance to see the face before the event was over.

I tried to convince myself that it was just a nightmare. Everything was fine—or so I thought. About a half hour later, there was a knock at my door. The duty rounds man told me that the block petty officer wanted to see me in the duty room on the second floor.

When I entered the room, he told me that he had gotten some bad news for me. He offered the phone for me to make the call to Victoria, British Columbia. I had a sinking feeling and walked out the door. I was in shock.

I called from a pay phone in the lobby. My father answered, and he told me that Warren was gone. I cried out in grief and sank to the floor. He would not tell me what had happened over the phone. I wanted to ask him if he took his own life, but I could not find the words. I wanted to believe that my vision had told me a lie.

I was sent to the sick bay while arrangements were made to fly me home for compassionate leave. I was prescribed antidepressants. Some of the questions I was asked about Warren by the base staff were a little disturbing. During my flight home, I remembered the Lord's Prayer. I repeated it in my mind. It gave me solace.

When I arrived home, my father told me what had happened. Warren had attached a garden hose to the exhaust pipe on the small blue car he drove and put the other end of it through the rear window. He then went for a drive on a trip that he would never return from. When he was found by the road with the motor still idling, it was too late. He had already expired.

This was a total shock for us all. How could someone like Warren have so much going for him and have something like this happen? I could not fathom what would drive Warren to the brink where he would even think of something like this; it just didn't make any sense to me. He was the last person that I could think of who would even think of suicide.

My father made me promise that I would never do what Warren did, and I complied. What mystified and shocked me about this news was how closely it paralleled my vision just after it happened. I never did tell my father or anyone else about it. This was something I would have to keep to myself . . . until now.

Chapter 6

The Movie

In 1978, I came home from my friend's house. I had just finished a night of playing in a musical band that my friends from Belmont Secondary School had put together. We had all the instruments, and I had an ear for listening to a song and figuring out which instrument was playing what without using a mixer.

I would show my friend Craig what the lead guitar was playing. My friend Scott played backup guitar. Russell played keyboards, and John was on the bass guitar. We played the Beatles, Pink Floyd, the Rolling Stones, and other popular rock groups. Later on, we would even come up with our own songs. If it wasn't for a traffic accident in my senior year that left me with a badly broken arm, we could have been a pretty good band—alas, it wasn't meant to be.

When I settled in front of the television in the rec room, I did my usual channel surfing before going to bed. That night, I came across a movie that caught my attention. It was a movie that had come out in 1971, but it had been produced when my father purchased the house in 1970. The name of the movie was *Willard*—there was also a sequel called *Ben*.[1]

It was about intelligent rats that were trained by Willard to do his bidding. The rats, led by Ben, turned on him in the end. One thing that caught my attention was that Willard used long wooden planks for the rats to run up and down. We had similar planks in our carport that I could use for Whiskers.

That weekend, I collected a few planks so that Whiskers could run up and down to the ledge that went around my room. I wouldn't have to keep picking him up to place on the ledge. He could join me while I was doing my homework whenever he wanted to.

The idea worked out beautifully. Whenever I entered my room, he would be up on the ledge or my desk because he couldn't make the jump to the ledge from the floor. I never saw him get on my bed—even though the distance from the ledge behind the headboard was only about a foot.

My copy of *Willard* is still my most cherished possession. When I served in the military, I had the option of flying out to Halifax for a course from British Columbia or taking holidays to drive to Halifax with a shipmate in his own car.

When I took the radar operator's course, I happened to come across *Willard* in a small video store! I couldn't believe it, and I had to get it. Cost did not matter to me, and I purchased it for sixty dollars.

If it wasn't for *Willard,* Whiskers would have been my last rat and I would have moved on. Whiskers passed away in November 1979, but I was left with a pretty neat setup in my bedroom. My parents often gave me strange looks about it, but I couldn't bear to take it all down. Finally, my mother got me another rat!

The new rat was the final piece to the puzzle. I was unaware at the time, but I was following my heart. I do not know what made my mom get this one because he wasn't beige like the others. He looked just like Ben so that became his name!

He was black with white-capped forepaws. The distinctive white patch on his belly resembled the one in the movie. This classified him as a Berkshire. I noticed that Ben was a different rat in the sequel. He was more of a solid black without the white-capped forepaws or the white patch on his belly. I wondered if anybody else noticed this.

I often wondered if the rat caught my mother's attention when she was looking for one to replace Whiskers. She had never seen the movie, but I had mentioned it to her.

I could not help but speculate that the groundwork for Ben's arrival was orchestrated from a higher power. Perhaps he was being used as a link by this higher order to perform his intended function.

Then again, this may have absolutely nothing to do with anything! I am simply leaving this open for contemplation and conjecture.

Chapter 7

My Brother Scott

Scott returned from Alberta because of a lack of good jobs and experience, eventually finding work as a delivery driver for the *Times Colonist* in Victoria. He delivered newspaper bundles for the paperboys to deliver. I guess this was kind of a promotion because he had been a delivery boy before I took over for him.

He held a number of jobs like working for a cartage business. He was quite the mechanic. He had an old Chevy Blazer with oversized tires that he was constantly taking apart and putting back together. The truck ran like new though. He still has it in North Surrey, but he never drives it anymore. He used to drive it often when he lived on Vancouver Island—and he even drove it in a few truck shows.

He would pick up his deliveries at midnight and go to his assigned route. He sometimes played a nasty prank on me when he got home around three in the morning. Just before going to bed, he would open my bedroom door and turn the thermostat all the way up to maximum.

I would wake up in a sweltering bedroom. I would open my window, turn the heat off, and get something to eat or drink while my bedroom cooled off. I wondered why this was happening until I heard him coming into the rec room.

It was dark, but there was enough light from the street lamp to see a silhouette of his arm poking around the door frame. I knew my thermostat had been turned all the way down before I went to bed.

I got out of bed, turned on the light, and saw that the thermostat was turned all the way up. Since he did not do it every night, I was at the mercy of when he was going to strike next. I guess you could call it sibling rivalry—that's just what brothers do.

Ben was one of the smartest rats that ever owned me. He lived up to his name and sure got a lot of use out of the ramps in my room.

On April 18, 1980, my dad gave me a big green garbage bag to take down stairs to the rec room to clean up the mess that Scott and I had left behind. We were the sole residents and had chores to do, and everybody got their turn. There were newspapers, pizza boxes, food containers, McDonald's containers, and other garbage.

I figured I would clean up my bedroom since the bag was only about three-quarters full. I emptied the wastebasket in my bedroom. Around dinnertime, my father called me up to set the table. I finished up in my bedroom, tossed the garbage bag aside, and headed up to set the table. When there is another job your parents want you to do, you pretty much drop what you are doing to complete later. Scott, Warren, Maggie, and I all took turns at setting the table and washing and drying the dishes.

Since it wasn't my turn for the dishes, I went straight to my friend's place to play a little music. Even though my friends and I were underage, we always had connections for getting some beers, having a few drinks, getting a little high, and jamming!

We had a pretty good night as usual. When I returned home, I was feeling no pain. I went straight to bed. I turned the lights on in the rec room, but didn't turn on my bedroom light. I got undressed, went to the washroom, and crawled into bed after turning off the rec room light.

Since there was no paper on Sunday, this was Scott's last night of work before the weekend. Even though he worked six nights a week, it did not pay that much. He only worked a few hours each night.

When Scott got home, he was up to his old pranks. He turned my thermostat all the way up before going to bed—no doubt having a chuckle or two along the way. I was fast asleep, passed right out, and dead to the world.

I suddenly came out of my sleep because of a scratching noise in my left ear. I could feel something cool and soft poking in my ear. I heard rapid breathing and something poking me in the ear over and over again.

I thought that a large animal had somehow gotten into my bedroom through my window, (although the window was closed) and started chewing on my head. I jumped up out of a deep, sound sleep and turned on my light. My main concern was for Ben. Was he in danger? Was he safe?

Ben was doing a crazy dance on my pillow. His eyes were bugged out, and he seemed to be agitated about something. I said, "What's the matter, little buddy? What's wrong?" He had never done this before. As my senses began to wake up, I noticed how warm it was in my bedroom. I was still a little groggy. It was not warm enough to wake me out of my sleep, but it was definitely noticeable.

I noticed a melting plastic smell. I looked toward the window and saw the bag of garbage from the previous evening! Ben was bobbing his head up and down as if he was pointing out the danger to me.

Jesus Christ, Scott! Are you trying to kill us all? I jumped out of bed and turned off the thermostat. I ran to the bedroom window, drew the curtains, and opened the window. I was in panic mode. When I pulled the bag away from the heater, there was a hole in the side of the bag as large as a beach ball.

Plastic dripped down to the strip of linoleum under the heater. I could see the plastic on top of the heat register boiling furiously like a liquid in a saucepan on the stove set to high. I could see little white puffs of smoke coming out of the bubbles as they burst—even after the heat was turned off.

I touched the puddle under the heat register. Big mistake! The molten liquid stuck to the tip of my finger. I whipped my hand around wildly in an attempt to get rid of what was burning me. This was from the floor—not from the top of the register where the plastic was much hotter. I had to stop whipping my hand around to peel the blob of plastic from my fingertip. It gave me a second degree burn in the form of a small blister which was really quite painful. Even after I turned off the heater and pulled away the bag, I thought that it was going to burst into flames!

I had forgotten exactly how I woke up. When I started to calm down, I threw the bag into the garbage like I should have in the first place, aired my bedroom out, and went back to sleep. It was 3:30 when I went back to bed, but I did not realize what had happened until I woke up later that morning.

When I woke up, I thought it was a nightmare. I detected the strong smell of plastic in the air. In the dim morning light, I could see a green streak on the baseboard heater cover. My left index finger still stung with pain. I started to piece together what transpired.

When I checked on Ben in his cage, it suddenly hit me. If it wasn't for Ben, we would all be dead—all of us. He got to me in a nick of time!

I realized that in just one more minute—two or three at the most—the bag would have burst into flames, setting my curtains on fire. I wouldn't have stood a chance. My parents, Warren, and Maggie were sleeping on the second floor.

I broke down—my head was spinning. *If it wasn't for you, Ben, we would all be dead. We would all be dead—and it would have been all my fault*! I nearly had a nervous breakdown. It was like somebody had taken a heavy sledge hammer and slugged me in the groin. My legs turned to rubber, and I couldn't stand up. I collapsed into a chair, shaking uncontrollably. It was an epiphany for me.

I knew the kind of pranks my brother was playing on me. It had been going on since Ben's arrival! Why wasn't I more careful about what I did with the garbage bag? How could I be so careless and irresponsible? This kind of thing was going to haunt me for the rest of my life. I often reflected on the night terrors and the ghostly vision of my grandmother.

I often wondered if he was genuinely concerned about me being in danger himself, or whether it was a self-preservation instinct. The danger was there—he was aware of it, and he used the ramps I set up in and around his cage to get to me. How odd that the ramps were available from the renovation.

Odder still was the fact that my bedroom was the only one with a ledge that went halfway around the room and made it feasible for me to set up these ramps. It would not have been possible in any other bedroom.

What if Scott and I had been in opposite bedrooms? He only took the added bedroom because he felt obligated to our father, as he was the oldest. If the added bedroom had been there when we moved in, he would have taken mine instead. What if I hadn't seen *Willard*? If any of these events was taken out of the picture or altered in any way, none of us would be here today. It was as if all of the pieces that led to our salvation had been put into place by a higher power.

I can't help but think that *Willard* was produced for me to see—through this higher order. Could it be that God was speaking to me through the rat?

I acquired this the day before Warren's passing! I remember showing it to my roommates in Halifax on the rented TV and VCR in our room before they left that weekend, in 1986. It is as though death felt cheated and took one of us as payment for what the rat took away from the specter of death itself! In exchange for the thing that was instrumental to our very salvation, death was punishing me by taking Warren. I would gladly trade it back for him, but a deal with death can never be undone.

I received information about a letter that Warren wrote to me shortly after I got the bad news. I wondered if it was in the form of a suicide note, but I will never know because of a freak fire at the post office.

His letter was in one of the mailbags that burned in the fire. I believe the powers that be did not want me to see it—for whatever reason. There must be a price to pay for divine intervention. I never will get closure on this.

Maybe it is best for me not to know what was in the letter. It could even have been part of the deal with death itself. Then again . . . this may have absolutely nothing to do with anything!

When this first happened, I wanted to tell the whole world what happened—along with all the strange coincidences that seemed to keep happening around the rat in my life and what a miracle this all was. However, it occurred to me that, if I did so, I would expose myself with the grievous errors that I committed that nearly destroyed us all.

I wasn't ready to tell the whole world that it was my fault—and how it took the loyalty of a beloved rat to correct my error, saving us all from death. I suspected that Scott had an idea of what happened because the plastic smell was present in my bedroom and the rec room over the next few days. He never did that kind of thing again.

Ben only woke me up this way twice. A month later, he woke me up at around the same time, in the same way. I panicked when he did this again! *What now? My bedroom wasn't on fire.* I got out of bed and looked through the whole house. Nobody had broken into the place; there were no floods, earthquakes, or tornadoes. What was next? When I went back to bed, I looked at Ben and said, "I hope you don't make a habit of doing this unless it's a real emergency! False alarm this time, my friend, but I know you mean well." I went back to sleep.

Ben was right after all! It was not any real danger to us, but I found out later that Mount St. Helens had blown its top! The shockwave rattled my bedroom window for a few seconds on Sunday, May 18, at around 7:50 in the morning.

It came back with increasing intensity and then suddenly dropped off again. Immediately after that, I heard a distant explosion that sounded like the world's largest cannon. The dissipating shockwaves that rattled my windows must have preceded the blast. It was no doubt a powerful explosion.

Ben must have detected these disturbances from deep within the earth with his superior sense of hearing—several hours before the event even took place from over two hundred miles away![2] It must have been this event that he was trying to warn me about. Rats truly are amazing animals! Instead of my family and me, he was protecting all who were in danger around the blast site. He just didn't know how to tell me—other than to get me up the way he did. Heck, I wouldn't even know how—even if he did. Nobody would believe me.

Years later, I found out about an aunt from my father's side lived in that area. Thankfully, she survived. I came to know and love her after her husband passed away.

I have often wondered if guardian angels truly do exist. After these amazing events took place, I came to know mine in the form of the rat. I truly do worship the animal.

Chapter 8

Some Rat Facts

Why the rat? Why not? The rat was pretty much an influence in my life from as far back as I could remember. I cannot help but feel connected to the animal in some way. Curiously, there is a whole industry that is dedicated to exterminating them.

They are not even allowed as pets in Alberta, but that unfortunate law did not take effect until many years after this event. Humankind's attempts to eradicate the animal from the face of the earth have been a failure. Rats are resilient survivors. If it wasn't for the rat's strong survival instincts, it would have been the death of me and my family. I got to know a lot more about the animal after these experiences.

For instance, they are worshipped in some parts of the world as deities. From my own experience, I can understand why! Rats are extremely loyal and intelligent and have a chain of command in their societal structure very much like ours—although they seem to make it work much better!

Priests at the rat temple outside of Pakistan believe that when a rat dies, it is reincarnated as a human. When a human dies, he or she is reincarnated as a rat! They believe that these rats house the spirits of their dead worshippers (kabbas) that have served them in a previous life as a human. Perhaps I was one of them.[3]

The rats inside the temple do not go out, and the rats outside do not come in. I found this interesting because whenever I moved into a residence with my rats—I kept this secret in the past because of other people's views of them, but I no longer do—I noticed that I never had a problem with outside rats. Even if there was a rat problem in the area, it always went away when I took up residence.

There was one exception in my experience. When I was residing in Coquitlam, I discovered a black roof rat living behind a work bench in the carport. I befriended her with treats that I left on a ledge by the workbench when I came home from work.

She eventually ventured into my residence in search of food, but she never went near my bedroom where I was keeping a number of rats. I got up one night to go to the bathroom, and I heard the sound of her little feet when she peeked around the corner in the hall.

The last time I saw her, she ran up to the ledge in the carport after I returned home from work to show off her children, following her out into the world, as if to say good-bye!

Because of the rats' high sensitivity to smell and hearing, they know of resident rats in the area, so they take up residence elsewhere. They may be the same species, but they are a different breed, like a wolf is to a coyote, a bear, or a fox. They are all canines. This is one of the many benefits to keeping them as pets.

A 2007 study found rats to possess Metacognition, a mental ability previously only documented in humans and some primates.[4] Due to their high intelligence, ingenuity, aggressiveness and adaptability, their psychology, in a lot of ways, are similar to ours. Perhaps this is why rats bond so easily with humans because we are very like minded. It also explains why they make such great survivors. Their ability to think, reason and problem solve.

An article in the Province newspaper on April 1, 2004, discusses genetics and the rat's genome. It was discovered that humans and rats have evolved from a common mammalian ancestor that existed some 80 million years ago, during the final reign of the dinosaurs![5] We sure have a lot in common with the rat. Mother Nature can often be a mad scientist when it comes to genetics!

Speaking of genetics, some rats have gone through a recent genetic mutation that gives them blue fur! The first blue rat was discovered in a pet shop in Southern California in the mid-nineties. [6] The first one I ever saw was a computer-generated version of one in a 2007 movie called *Ratatouille*! I thought the color was pure fiction, like the characters in the movie.

It reminded me of a dream I had in the early eighties, around the time when these unusual events continued to unfold in my life. They say you can't dream in color, but this one was different. I was walking along this trail in the forest, enjoying the scenery and the walk. It started out to be a pleasant dream that gradually turned into a nightmare.

It was getting darker out, and I wandered off the trail. I could not find it, and I was desperately stumbling through the thick underbrush for what seemed like hours. Exhausted, frightened, and weak, I ended up breaking through a thicket into a small clearing.

In the middle of the clearing was an old tree stump. The moonlight was shining onto the tree stump through a clearing in the forest. There was something sitting on top of it. As I approached, it appeared to be a rat. I could see the outline of its fur silhouetted by the moonlight, and I could see a bright dark-blue tinge in its outline.

He turned to me and told me his name was Blue Beard and he would help me find my way out of the forest. As he guided me in the right direction, he mentioned that we would meet again. I wondered what he meant by that as I was awakening from this dream.

A blue rat? That's almost as absurd as a talking rat! I simply dismissed it from my mind and thought nothing of it until I saw a real one for the first time. It absolutely blew me away! When are they going to develop the power of speech? They already have in their own way.

They can tell each other about danger, what foods are okay to eat, and they can even laugh! You need special bat detector transducers to bring the frequency of their laughter down to a level where human hearing, one of our limited senses, can hear it.[7] I recently saw a documentary on television titled "Rat Genius" that demonstrated how they can do this.

Rats are gaining popularity and recognition throughout the world for their unique abilities. I have seen videos of rat shows in Russia. They are a very popular pet in Australia, the Western United States, the UK, and Canada.

I recently became a member of a rat fancier group called RatsPacNW, who talk about their rats. I acquired two Russian Blue males from the Nampa Rat Rescue through them. Since they were my first blue rats, I named one of them Ratatouille after the very first rat I saw. I named his brother Blue Beard from the one in my dream years ago—before they even existed!

The remarkable thing about Blue Beard is his markings. He has the same white capped forepaws and a similar white patch on his belly like the rat in Willard. The only difference is that he is blue! Could Ben and Blue Beard be one and the same? After I adopted them there was a surge of unusual events that followed.

I went to my first rat show in New Westminster, British Columbia, on February 12, 2011; it happened to be in a hall where my company's union used to hold our union meetings! I couldn't even begin to figure the odds of something like this! Instead of the faces of my union brothers, I was looking at lots of rats and the people who love them, competing for various events that were presented at the show. This was a surreal experience for me!

There are even rat parties. I have already been to a few. They are normally held by individuals who run ratteries. A group of people will get together and bring snacks and treats—not only for ourselves, but for our small furry friends as well. They are held for the purpose of viewing and handling the babies, called kittens, for people who have an interest in adopting them.

The adult rats are there to handle as well, but a number of them are used for breeding purposes—or favorites of the caretakers—and are not up for adoption. There is a strict adoption policy put into place for these animals—not everybody qualifies, only the elite.

I was bemused to discover that there is even a day dedicated to rats called World Rat Day! It is on April 4 every year. This date was chosen through an Internet site called the Rat List. It is the longest running site that is dedicated to rats and the people who have them; it was founded on that date.

Every two years, the company that I work for has its employees re-certified to use the machines to do their job. I happened to be re-certified on World Rat Day! I did not choose this date—it just happened to fall on it! I have the equipment operator's card that bears the date.

What surprises me about the date is it takes place precisely two weeks before the anniversary of the event that changed my life forever. The first rat show I attended, dubbed Ratstravaganza, took place precisely two weeks before my forty-eighth birthday! It was also the first time the show took place at this hall.

Due to the Winter Olympics that took place the previous year, the show for 2010 had to be cancelled. Due to scheduling and other factors that came into play, the show could not be held at a church hall where it was annually scheduled, so the 8th annual show was held at this hall. What is even more remarkable is that these BC Rat Shows were taking place for as long as I worked at my present employment, eight years!

Rats also enjoy the distinction of being the number one animal in the Chinese zodiac which consists of twelve animals in its twelve year cycle. According to the story, the rat used its cunningness and intelligence to win the race and came in first! All the others followed the rat.

Rats are also being recognized for the tremendous benefit that they have on humankind. There is a group of individuals operating out of Africa called Hero Rats.[8] They were actually scheduled to show up at Ratstravaganza. Their table was right next to mine, but they were a no show. I would have really liked to meet them.

Their goal is to train these large African Pouched Rats to sniff out landmines that can't be located by metal detectors due to the nonmetallic components that are used.

They help clear out landmines in fields, ravaged by war that can be used for farming, giving families a chance to develop a normal way of life and making this a better world for all.

They are also trained to detect harmful diseases in their early stages, such as pulmonary tuberculosis, that puts modern science to shame. For every twenty cases that human efforts can find, these rats can do two thousand! I find it interesting that rats are being used to save human lives, but not quite in the same way that mine saved us! There is much more about them that could fill several more pages if I were to continue.

When I reflect upon my life and the continuing circumstances around these unusual events that keep unfolding in my life around the rat, I am aware of something that continues to amaze me. How can I explain these events if they will always be a mystery to me? I may be reading too much into this, but my only conclusion is that our lives are preordained. Mine just happens to be ordained around the rat. Why? I do not know. All I know is that I have been—and always will be—the rat worshipper.

You are probably thinking that this was all pure coincidence. I may agree, but there is a lot to be said about the unknown. My first encounter with the rat set into motion a chain of events that affected the outcome of my life. The rat paid me back for the water I gave it when it introduced itself to me long ago, by giving me gifts of far greater value—like my niece Jessica—that continues to this day and forever after.

If ever there was a purpose for the rat in this world, then it has served its purpose . . . by making a difference in my life and the lives of so many others . . . by showing me my purpose and sharing with others what it has done for me.

The rat rules! Then again . . . well, you know.

References

1. *Willard*: 1970 A Bing Crosby production. Printed in U.S.A. Released 1971.

2 Sound travels at 768 MPH. The explosion at Mt. Saint Helens took place at 7:32.17 on the morning on May 18, 1980. It would take just under sixteen minutes for the sound to travel 200 miles, making it around 7:50 in the morning.

3. The information about the rat temple can be viewed in a YouTube video called "Rat Temple in India." A temple in Deshnok, India, is devoted to the worship of rats.

4. Rat: Wikipedia Encyclopedia. Subtitle: As subjects of scientific research.

5. The source for the article "The rat undergoes the ultimate dissection" was taken from microfiche information in *The Province* newspaper from the Surrey Library records in Surrey, British Columbia.

6. AFRMA—The Blue Rat—The first Blue to be discovered in Southern California by an AFRMA member was a little female hooded. She was found in a pet shop in the mid ninties.

7. Rat laughter – You Tube: subject— can rats laugh? From Tierney Lab.

8. Frontlineworld Tanzania — Hero Rats. Story Synopsis and Video, PBS.